A New True Book

CONGRESS

By Carol Greene

CHILDRENS PRESS ™

CHICAGO

Meeting room of the Senate Foreign
Relations committee

Library of Congress Cataloging in Publication Data

Greene, Carol.
    The new true book of Congress.
    (Includes index)

    Summary: Describes the structure, function, and
interrelationship of the two houses of Congress.
    1. United States. Congress—Juvenile literature.
[1. United States. Congress] I. Title.
JK1064.G65   1985   328.73   84-23243
ISBN 0-516-01939-2   AACR2

TABLE OF CONTENTS

The United States Congress meets in the Capitol in Washington, D.C.

CONGRESS AND THE CONSTITUTION

The most important laws in the United States are in the Constitution. The Constitution says that the United States must have a Congress. The job of Congress is to make laws.

The Constitution says that the president of the United States must carry out the laws that Congress makes.

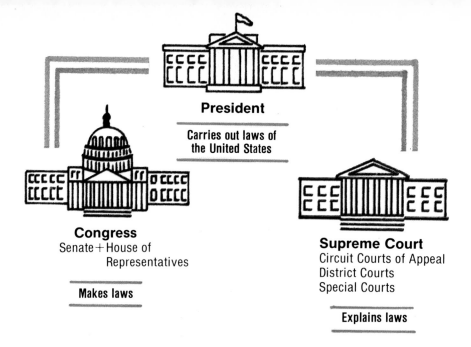

President

Carries out laws of
the United States

Congress
Senate + House of
Representatives

Makes laws

Supreme Court
Circuit Courts of Appeal
District Courts
Special Courts

Explains laws

It says that the Supreme
Court and other lower
courts must explain these
laws.

Each part of the United
States government must do
its own job and nobody
else's, says the Constitution.
That way no part will have

As president of the United States, Ronald Reagan (left) has the power to appoint people to serve on the Supreme Court (right).

too much power. This separation of work is called a balance of power.

The president cannot make laws. The Supreme Court cannot make laws. Only Congress can make laws.

The Constitution says Congress must have two

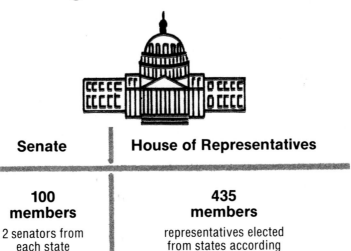

The Congress of the United States

Senate	House of Representatives
100 members	**435 members**
2 senators from each state	representatives elected from states according to population

parts. These are called houses. One house is the Senate. The other is the House of Representatives. All the laws made for the United States must be approved by both the Senate and the House of Representatives.

THE SENATE

The Senate is one house of Congress. Voters in each of the fifty states elect two people to send to the Senate. That makes one hundred senators in all.

Senators serve for six years. This is called a term. They can serve for as many terms as they like, as long as the people in their home states go on electing them.

A senator must be at least thirty years old and must have been a U.S. citizen for at least nine years. Each senator must live in the state that chooses him or her.

The Constitution gives the Senate some special jobs. No one else may do these jobs.

Wide-angle view of the United States Senate

The Senate must say
yes or no to any treaties
the president makes. It
also must say yes or no to
people the president
chooses, such as cabinet
officers, Supreme Court
justices, and ambassadors.

In 1868 the Senate acted as a court of impeachment for the trial of President Andrew Johnson. President Johnson escaped conviction by a single vote.

A government official who does something very bad can lose his or her job. It doesn't happen often. But when it does, the Senate holds the trial.

For his or her work a senator is paid $69,800 a year.

THE HOUSE OF REPRESENTATIVES

The other house of Congress is the House of Representatives. There are 435 representatives in the House. Each state chooses its own representatives.

The number of representatives elected from a state depends on the number of people who live in the state. A state with many people gets to

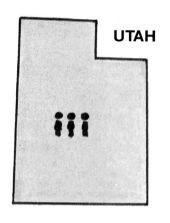

UTAH

NEW YORK

elect many representatives. (New York elects thirty-four representatives.) A state with fewer people gets to elect fewer representatives. (Utah has three.)

Representatives serve for two-year terms. They can be elected again and again, just like senators.

Wide-angle view of the United States House of Representatives

They are paid $69,800 for their work.

Representatives must be at least twenty-five years old. They must have been U.S. citizens for at least seven years. And each must live in the state that elects him or her.

The Constitution gives the House of Representatives special jobs, too.

Only the House can start laws that make people pay taxes.

If a government official does something very bad, only the representatives can decide whether or not to put that person on trial before the Senate.

Congress begins regular session on January 3.
The session usually ends in July.

WHEN AND WHERE

Congress meets once every year. The Constitution says it must do this.

This meeting is called a regular session. It usually lasts from January 3 until

The reflecting pool mirrors the Capitol building.

July 31. But sometimes it goes on into fall.

If there is an emergency, the president can call a special session of Congress.

Congress meets in the Capitol in Washington, D.C. Each house has its own meeting hall in the big

CAPITOL FLOOR PLAN

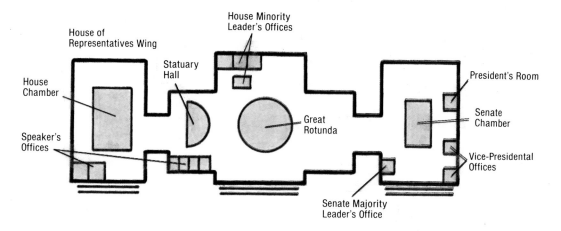

House Minority
Leader's Offices

House of
Representatives Wing

Statuary
Hall

House
Chamber

President's Room

Great
Rotunda

Senate
Chamber

Speaker's
Offices

Vice-Presidental
Offices

Senate Majority
Leader's Office

building. These halls are
called chambers.

Most of the time the two
houses meet separately.
But sometimes they meet
together. This is called a
joint session.

Senators and representatives
hold a joint session when

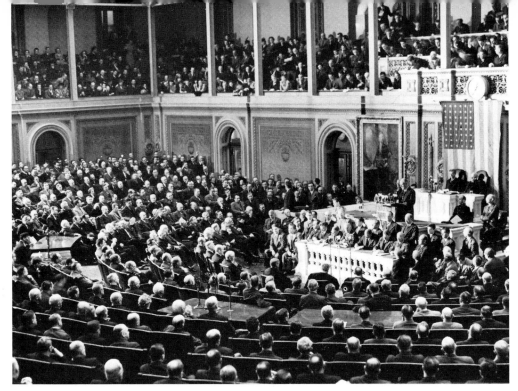

On December 8, 1941 President Franklin Delano Roosevelt addressed a joint session of Congress asking for a declaration of war against Japan.

the president wants to speak
to them. They meet to look
at and count the votes after
every presidential election.
But they never make laws
in a joint session.

THE MOST IMPORTANT JOB

The most important job of Congress is to make laws. But it can't make just any laws. The Constitution tells what kind of laws Congress can make.

Only Congress can make laws about taxes and borrowing money. Only Congress can declare war and make coins and paper

When Congress (right) considers passing a new law it hears from people who support the law and from people who are against the law. In 1871 Victoria Claflin Woodhull (left) asked the Judiciary Committee of the House of Representatives to support the law granting women the right to vote. Seated directly behind Mrs. Woodhull is Elizabeth Cady Stanton. Susan B. Anthony is at the extreme left of the picture.

money. Only Congress can make some laws about national defense and set up courts that are lower than the Supreme Court. It also makes some laws about business or trade in the United States and with foreign countries.

The Constitution says that Congress can make the laws needed to carry out other laws.

For example, suppose Congress makes a law that says people must wear seat belts. Then it can make another law that says what will happen if people *don't* wear seat belts.

There are nine justices of the Supreme Court, from left to right, Associate Justices Thurgood Marshall, John P. Stevens, William J. Brennan, Lewis F. Powell, Chief Justice Warren E. Burger, Associate Justices William H. Rehnquist, Byron R. White, Sandra Day O'Connor, Harry A. Blackmun.

Congress may not make any law that disagrees with the Constitution. If it does, the Supreme Court can throw that law out.

HOW A LAW IS MADE

A law can begin in the Senate or in the House of Representatives. At that time it is called a bill.

Suppose Senator Smith wants a new law to protect wild animals. She knows her voters back home want that law, too.

So she talks to experts. Then she writes the bill. She has copies made for all the other senators.

Next Senator Smith's bill goes to a Senate standing committee. Members of the committee can do one of three things after studying the bill.

They can send the bill back to the Senate with no changes. They can make changes in the bill and send it back. Or they can table the bill. (That means let it sit and take no action.)

Suppose they do send it

A senate hearing involves many witnesses and long hours of research.

Standing Committees of Congress

Senate	House of Representatives
Agriculture, Nutrition, and Forestry	Agriculture
Appropriations	Appropriations
Armed Services	Armed Services
Banking, Housing, and Urban Affairs	Banking, Finance, and Urban Affairs
Budget	Budget
Commerce, Science, and Transportation	District of Columbia
Energy and Natural Resources	Education and Labor
Environment and Public Works	Foreign Affairs
Finance	Government Operations
Foreign Relations	House Administration
Governmental Affairs	Interior and Insular Affairs
Judiciary	Interstate and Foreign Commerce
Labor and Human Resources	Judiciary
Rules and Administration	Merchant Marine and Fisheries
Veterans' Affairs	Post Office and Civil Service
	Public Works and Transportation
	Rules
	Science and Technology
	Small Business
	Standards of Official Conduct
	Veterans' Affairs
	Ways and Means

back with no changes. Then it goes on the Senate's calendar. One day it comes up for a vote. Over half the senators (fifty-one people) must vote yes to pass it.

If the senators do pass the bill, it goes on to the House of Representatives. At first it must go to a House committee. The committee studies it. Then the representatives vote. Over half of them (218 representatives) must vote yes.

If the bill passes both the Senate and the House of Representatives, the bill goes to the president. If

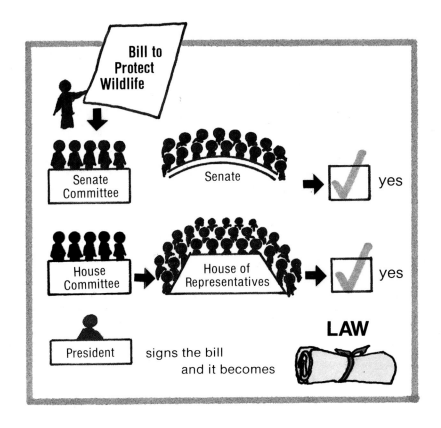

the president signs it, it becomes a law. If the president doesn't sign it for ten days, it becomes a law anyway.

President Reagan signs the law that made Martin Luther King's birthday a national holiday.

Sometimes the president vetoes a bill. A veto is like a big NO. It means that the president does not want the bill to become a law.

If the president vetoes Senator Smith's bill, that's not the end of it. It can still become a law. But two-thirds of the senators and two-thirds of the representatives must vote for it this time.

Representative Jones could start a bill just as Senator Smith did. But his bill would go to the House of Representatives first. Then it would go to the Senate.

Senator John Tower

Senators and representatives hold hearings and discuss new bills. Normally they meet separately. However, they may call a joint committee meeting to solve some problems.

PROBLEMS WITH BILLS

Sometimes bills run into problems. People on the committees might want to change the bills. These changes are called amendments. Someone might want to change Senator Smith's bill so it protects fish as well as wild animals.

Sometimes the Senate and the House cannot agree on what a bill

Engraving showing Senator Henry Clay presenting a compromise law to the Senate in 1850.

should say. Then a few senators and a few representatives get together to work out the problems.

It takes time and hard work to make a law. That is to make sure only good laws will be made.

President Roosevelt asked Congress to declare war on Japan in 1941.

OTHER JOBS

Congress has other jobs, too. These are in the Constitution.

Only Congress can declare war.

Congress can investigate certain things. Suppose they think the FBI is doing a bad job. They might decide to check into it.

Congress gives the president and the president's workers money to do their jobs. So Congress can make them explain how they will use this money.

Suppose the president is hurt in a car crash. Congress must make sure he or she can still do the job. If not, the vice-president should take over.

Vice-president George Bush (left) would replace Ronald Reagan if the president should die or be unable to do his job.

The Women's Christian Temperance Union (above) wanted to outlaw the sale of alcoholic beverages in the United States.
This law was passed in the Eighteenth Amendment in 1919. But the law was unpopular and was overturned by the Twenty-first Amendment, passed in 1933.

Congress can even change the Constitution. But that is hard to do. At least two-thirds of the states must agree with the change.

Representatives and senators go to many

In order to be elected to office politicians march in parades and give speeches asking for public votes. Representative Dan Rostenkowski (left, in center of picture) and Representative Geraldine Ferraro (right) ran for election in 1984. Rostenkowski won. Ferraro, the first woman to run for vice-president of the United States, lost.

committee meetings in Washington. They travel a lot, too. Sometimes they give speeches. They find out things for their committees. They help with special ceremonies.

People in Congress have some special rights. These are to help them do their jobs better.

For example, they cannot be arrested while they are serving in Congress, unless they do something very bad, such as murder someone or tell government secrets to an enemy.

But their own house can throw them out if they are a terrible senator or representative.

Office of the Speaker of the House of Representatives (left).
Representative Hyde's office in Illinois.

THE PEOPLE BACK HOME

Most representatives and senators have one office in Washington and one in their home state. They need these two offices to do a good job.

Representative Hyde campaigning for office

People in Congress must spend a lot of time listening to people back home. They are representing these people. If they make too many laws that the people don't like, they might not get elected again.

It is the job of the voters back home to tell

Senator Paul Simon shakes a voter's hand and asks for his vote.

representatives and
senators what they think.
They should write letters or
make phone calls. Most
people in Congress hold
meetings back home, too.
They *want* to know what
the voters think.

AN IDEA THAT WORKS

Sometimes Congress has
problems. It may run out
of money. It may argue too
much with the president.
Or senators and
representatives may argue
too much with each other.

But even with its
problems, the whole idea
of Congress works. It lets

the people of the United
States have a lot to say
about their government. It
makes the United States a
better, stronger country.

WORDS YOU SHOULD KNOW

ambassador(am•BASS•uh•der)—an important person who represents the government of one country in another country

amendment(uh•MEND•ment)—a change or addition made to a law or bill

bill(BILL)—a draft, or early version, of a proposed law

cabinet(KAB•ih•net)—a group of people who help the president. Cabinet members also are in charge of governmental departments.

chambers(CHAIM•burz)—halls used as meeting places for legislative or judicial groups

law(LAW)—a rule or action passed by a legislature that is to be observed and obeyed by all the people in a nation or group

session(SESH•un)—a meeting or series of meetings of a group of lawmakers

standing committee(STAN•ding kuh•MITT•ee)—a small, permanent group of legislators that studies and reports on one specific type of possible legislation

table(TAY•bil)—to remove a bill from study or consideration for an indefinite time

term(TIRM)—the length of time for which a person is elected to serve in a specific office

treaties(TREET•eez)—agreements signed by the representatives of two or more nations

veto(VEET•oh)—the power of the president to keep a law passed by Congress from going into effect. A veto can be bypassed if Congress passes the law again by a two-thirds vote.

INDEX

About the author

Carol Greene has degrees in English literature and musicology. She has worked in international exchange programs as an editor and as a teacher. She now lives in St. Louis, Missouri and writes full-time. She has had published over fifty books—most of them for children. Other Childrens Press books by Ms. Greene include England, Poland, Japan, *and* Yugoslavia *(in the Enchantment of the World series);* Marie Curie *and* Louisa May Alcott *(in the People of Distinction series);* Holidays Around the World, Robots, Music, Language, The United Nations, Astronauts, Presidents, *and* The Supreme Court *(in the True Book series);* The Thirteen Days of Halloween; A Computer Went A-Courting; *and* Sandra Day O'Connor: First Woman on the Supreme Court.